The Food Cycle

by David Smith

Illustrations by John Yates

Wayland

Titles in the series

The Human Cycle
The Food Cycle
The Plant Cycle
The Water Cycle

Words printed in **bold** can be found
in the glossary on page 30.

This edition published in 1997 by
Wayland Publishers Ltd

First published in 1993 by
Wayland Publishers Ltd
61 Western Road, Hove
East Sussex BN3 1JD

British Library Cataloguing in Publication Data
Smith, David
    Food Cycle. – (Natural Cycles Series)
    I. Title II. Yates, John III. Series 612
    641.3

HARDBACK ISBN 0-7502-0740-X

PAPERBACK ISBN 0-7502-2125-9

Series Editor: Kathryn Smith
Series Designers: Robert Wheeler and Loraine Hayes

Typeset by Dorchester Typesetting Group Ltd
Printed and bound in Italy by G. Canale & C.S.p.A.

Contents

Food for life

We all have favourite foods. Perhaps your favourite is chocolate, or ice-cream. Maybe you prefer juicy fresh fruit. But food is more than something nice to eat. Our bodies need food. We cannot live without it.

Why do we need food?

Imagine your body is a factory. The **vital organs** inside you, such as your heart and lungs, are like the factory machines. The skin and bones of your body are like the bricks and cement of the factory walls, protecting the vital organs. The fuel which gives you the energy to keep the machines working is food. Food also supplies the building blocks needed to build a strong, healthy body.

We all need food to survive. Food gives us the energy to breathe and move – to live, in fact.

Have you ever thought how much fun it would be if you could eat just your favourite food . . . all day, every day? This might sound good, but nothing could be further from the truth. Your body must have a variety of different types of food, if you want to be healthy.

The food cycle

ABOVE Most plants, like this beautiful sunflower, use energy from the rays of the Sun to help make their own food. The plants' green leaves trap the energy from the Sun.

All living things need food; to grow, to repair damage and for energy.

Plants make their own food by mixing different ingredients. They take in water and **mineral salts** from the soil, and **carbon dioxide** from the air. The plants' green leaves trap light energy from the Sun, and use it to help turn the ingredients into sugars and **starches**, which are needed for energy and growth. This process of making food is called photosynthesis.

The goodness and energy made by photosynthesis is passed on to animals when they eat plants. Some animals get their food by eating only plants, and are called herbivores.

Sheep are herbivores. This means that they eat only plants.

The Food Cycle

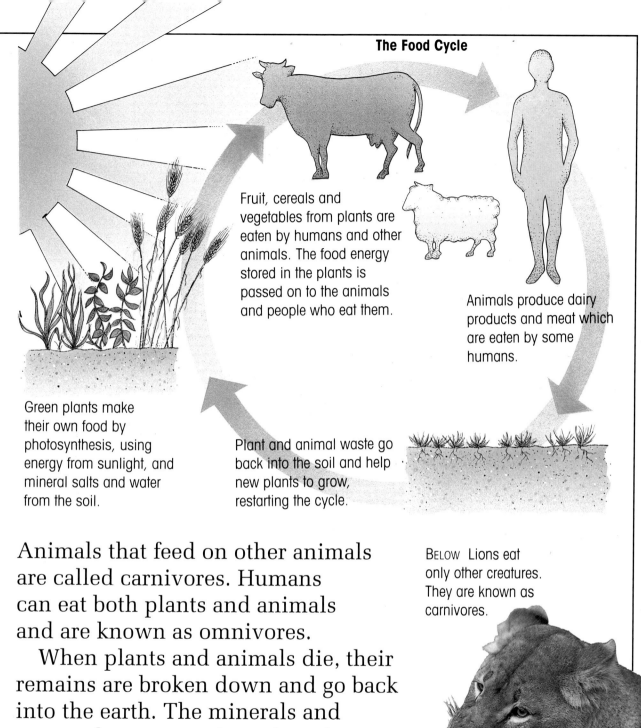

Fruit, cereals and vegetables from plants are eaten by humans and other animals. The food energy stored in the plants is passed on to the animals and people who eat them.

Animals produce dairy products and meat which are eaten by some humans.

Green plants make their own food by photosynthesis, using energy from sunlight, and mineral salts and water from the soil.

Plant and animal waste go back into the soil and help new plants to grow, restarting the cycle.

Animals that feed on other animals are called carnivores. Humans can eat both plants and animals and are known as omnivores.

When plants and animals die, their remains are broken down and go back into the earth. The minerals and energy they were using when they were alive go back into the soil, too. This goodness is taken up by plants and used to help them grow. In this way, the food cycle starts again.

BELOW Lions eat only other creatures. They are known as carnivores.

What's in a meal?

The next time you eat a meal, take a look at what foods are in front of you. We can put foods into different groups. Every day we should try to eat foods from each different group, if we are to give our bodies everything they need to stay healthy. Let's take a look at this packed lunch.

The wholemeal bread of the sandwich contains carbohydrates and fibre. The carbohydrates give us energy. Fibre helps to keep our digestive systems working well.

Bread and Cereals
eg: Brown bread
Bread rolls
Rice
Cornflakes
Bran

Fats and Oils
eg: Fish oil
Olive oil
Sunflower oil
Margarines

Orange juice

Tuna and fish oil

The orange juice contains vitamin c, which helps to firm our skin, and to keep our hair, eyes and teeth healthy.

The tuna in the sandwich contains proteins. Proteins are used to build up our bodies. Meat, cheese and **pulses** contain protein too.

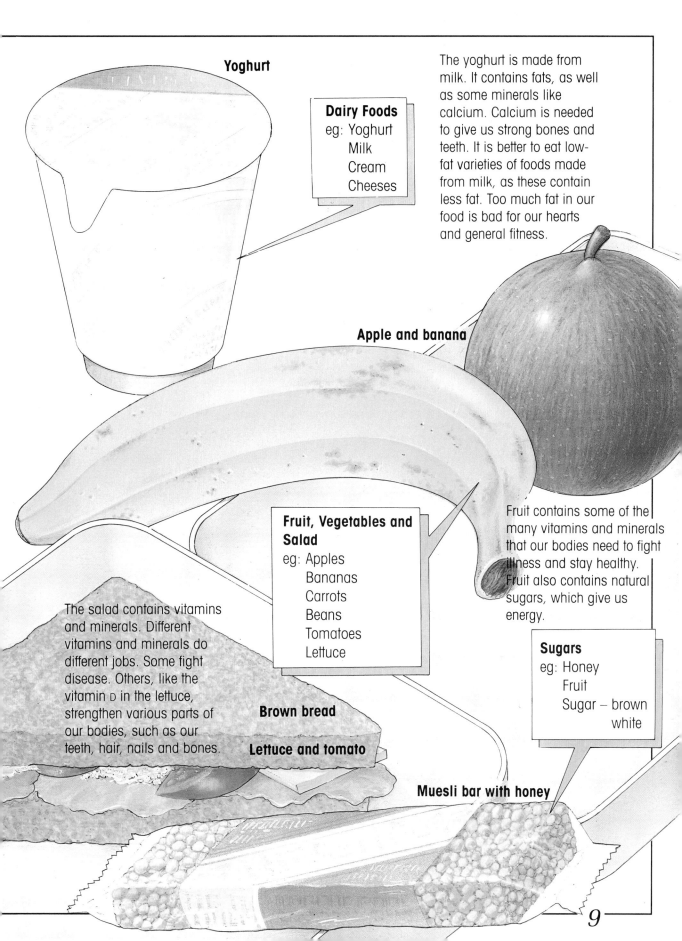

Yoghurt

The yoghurt is made from milk. It contains fats, as well as some minerals like calcium. Calcium is needed to give us strong bones and teeth. It is better to eat low-fat varieties of foods made from milk, as these contain less fat. Too much fat in our food is bad for our hearts and general fitness.

Dairy Foods
eg: Yoghurt
     Milk
     Cream
     Cheeses

Apple and banana

Fruit contains some of the many vitamins and minerals that our bodies need to fight illness and stay healthy. Fruit also contains natural sugars, which give us energy.

Fruit, Vegetables and Salad
eg: Apples
     Bananas
     Carrots
     Beans
     Tomatoes
     Lettuce

The salad contains vitamins and minerals. Different vitamins and minerals do different jobs. Some fight disease. Others, like the vitamin D in the lettuce, strengthen various parts of our bodies, such as our teeth, hair, nails and bones.

Brown bread

Lettuce and tomato

Sugars
eg: Honey
     Fruit
     Sugar – brown
               white

Muesli bar with honey

9

Where in the world?

The food we eat comes from all over the world and is grown in many different **climates**. Find out where different foods come from by reading food packaging labels and displays in supermarkets. Use this map to help look up which foods are grown in countries with different climates.

These sockeye salmon live in the cold waters off British Colombia.

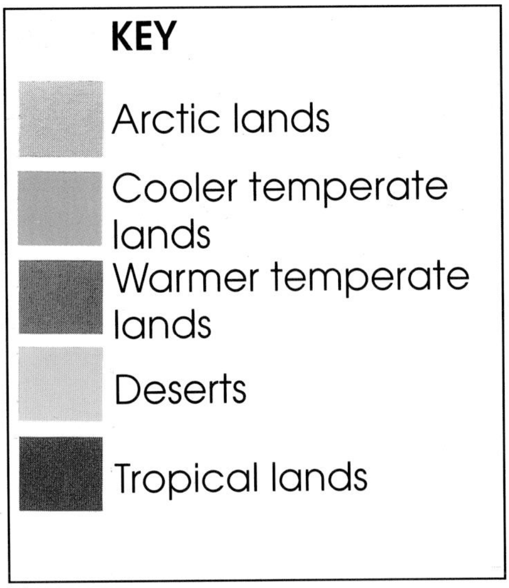

KEY

Arctic lands

Cooler temperate lands

Warmer temperate lands

Deserts

Tropical lands

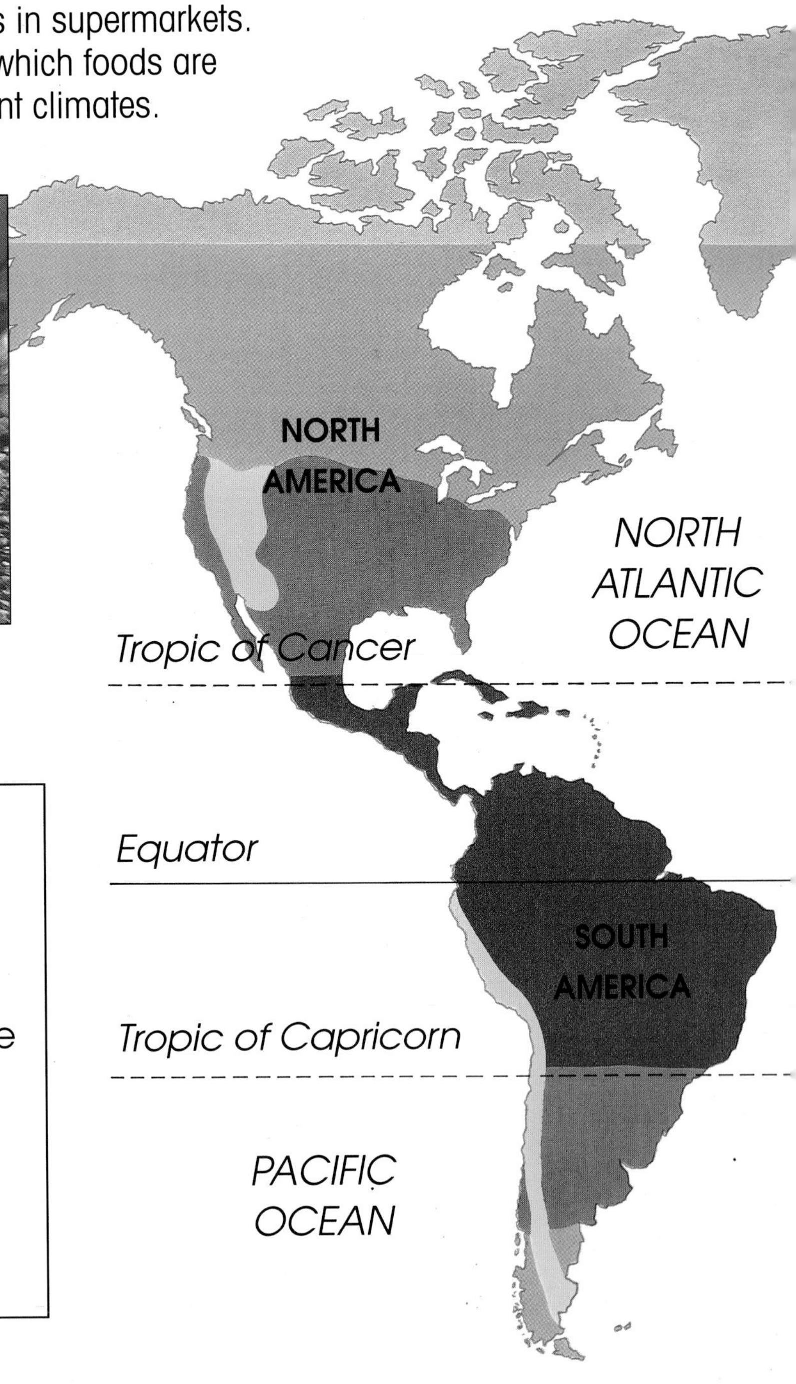

NORTH AMERICA

NORTH ATLANTIC OCEAN

Tropic of Cancer

Equator

SOUTH AMERICA

Tropic of Capricorn

PACIFIC OCEAN

RIGHT These delicious red apples are grown in the cool temperate lands of northern Europe.

BELOW These dates are grown in the dry climate of Israel.

ARCTIC OCEAN

EUROPE

ASIA

AFRICA

PACIFIC OCEAN

INDIAN OCEAN

SOUTH ATLANTIC OCEAN

AUSTRALASIA

LEFT
The hot wet climate of Sri Lanka is ideal for growing tea.

Is it fresh?

These lemons are growing in Ojai, California, USA. Usually lemons are picked when they are still slightly green and unripe. By the time they arrive in the shops they will be just ripe enough to eat.

Most people in this country buy their food from shops, markets and supermarkets. There is an amazing selection to choose from. Before we buy food, a lot of effort is made to make sure it reaches us in the best possible condition.

When fruit and vegetables have just been harvested, or when animals have just been slaughtered (killed), they are called fresh foods. It is healthy to eat fresh foods, because they still

Garden peas, fresh from the pod! Freshly picked fruit and vegetables often have far more taste than those which have been frozen or tinned. Food which has been tinned also loses some of its goodness.

Bacteria and fungi in the air have caused the tangerine at the front of this picture to grow mould. Fruit and vegetables should be stored in a clean, dry place, in order to make them last as long as possible.

contain all their natural goodness and flavour.

However, as soon as fresh food has been harvested or slaughtered, it starts to change. **Chemicals** inside the food start to make it decay, and tiny living things called **bacteria** and **fungi** start to grow. All these things can spoil the taste of the food. The bacteria and fungi also start to make toxins, or poisons, which would give us food poisoning if we ate them.

Using the cold

Food producers can do many things to make sure that fresh food is at its best when it reaches the shops. The lorry in this picture is **refrigerated**, to keep fresh the meat it is carrying to the shops.

Bacteria and fungi spread quickly when food is kept in warm places. If the food is kept in colder conditions, the spread of decay and the growth of bacteria and fungi is slowed down. For this reason food is often transported to, stored and displayed in shops in refrigerated containers.

Refrigeration does not keep food fresh for really long periods of time. Other methods are used to stop decay and bacteria spoiling the food. Freezing is an excellent way of keeping food unspoilt. It stops the number of bacteria from growing and prevents decay by turning the water in food to solid ice. Food is frozen at **temperatures** between −7°C and −23°C. The lower the temperature, the longer the food will last. Not all foods can be frozen. Some foods, such as tomatoes and lettuce, are damaged by the ice and go soft and shapeless when they thaw.

At home we can keep food fresh for longer by putting it in a fridge. Without fridges, we would have to shop for fresh food every day.

Using heat

The oldest way to preserve food uses heat from the Sun. For thousands of years people have hung meat, fish, and sometimes fruit, to dry in the heat of the Sun.

Tinned foods are **preserved** using heat. Food is put in **sterile** tins, which are sealed and put under steam. The steam is very hot – about 120°C – and kills any bacteria. Sometimes the food is put into bottles or jars. The sealed containers protect the food from bacteria in the air. Food preserved in this way loses some of its goodness. However, tinned or bottled food can stay fit to eat for up to two years!

See for yourself

You will need some fruit, screw-top containers, sugar, salt, vinegar, water, teaspoons and some polythene bags.

1. Fill one jar with water, one with vinegar, one with brine and one with sugar solution. Label each jar.

2. Place some pieces of chopped fruit in each jar and close the lid. Then cover each jar with a polythene bag.

3. Keep a diary over several weeks, of how the fruit changes in appearance. Which jars appear to preserve the fruit the best? For health and safety reasons, **do not** taste the food.

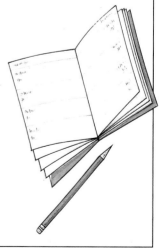

4. If you want to investigate further, with the help of an adult, try boiling the fruit first. Does this affect the speed of decay? Make the brine and sugar solutions stronger. Do they work better if they are stronger?

Food additives

OPPOSITE These women are checking the quality of potato crisps in the factory, before they are put into bags. Crisps are a kind of processed food. You can find out which additives are added to crisps by checking the ingredient label on their bag.

BELOW All of this food has been processed in some way. This means that additives have been added to alter either the look, taste or feel of the food.

Much of the food we eat is fresh and natural. This means that, when we buy it, the food has changed very little since it was harvested.

Other foods, like the ones in the picture below, are different. They have natural ingredients in them, but they are produced in factories by food companies. These foods have chemicals called additives in them.

All foods contain some natural chemicals. Additives, however, are chemicals which have been put into food by people.

Food additives do many jobs. Some are preservatives which stop the food spoiling. Others, such as sweeteners and flavourings, make the food taste different. Artificial colourings are used to make the food look brighter and more attractive.

Although additives often make food look and taste better, they certainly do not make the food more healthy. Some people prefer to eat natural food, as too many additives can be bad for us.

Preparing and cooking a meal

Preparing and cooking food is something only humans do. With imagination and a little effort we can come up with recipes that are both tempting and healthy. This delicious-looking milkshake has been made with fresh strawberries, semi-skimmed milk, yoghurt and low fat cream.

Cooking food to make a meal is something that only humans do. No other animal does this.

Cooking does several things to food. It makes some foods taste better and more pleasant to eat. Tough vegetables like potatoes and turnips are softened when they are cooked, and so can be digested more easily.

Cooking food also helps to **destroy** harmful bacteria. However, if food is cooked for too long, much of the goodness it contains is also destroyed. It is a good idea to steam vegetables rather than boil them, as this destroys fewer **nutrients**. Some foods like fresh fruit or salads are eaten raw, but they must be washed before they are eaten to remove dirt or chemicals.

LEFT Many vitamins and minerals are found just beneath the skin of fruit and vegetables. When we remove the skin by peeling, we also remove these precious nutrients.

BELOW Germs can breed very easily in a warm kitchen. It is extremely important to clean the kitchen regularly and to make sure that the cutlery and plates we use are clean too.

Keeping food clean is very important. Food should always be stored in a cool, clean, dry place before it is cooked. When we prepare food for cooking, we must make sure that the work surfaces and the knives we use are all clean, too.

Looking after food in this way is called being **hygienic**. It is an important way to stop harmful bacteria spreading disease, and to keep ourselves fit and healthy!

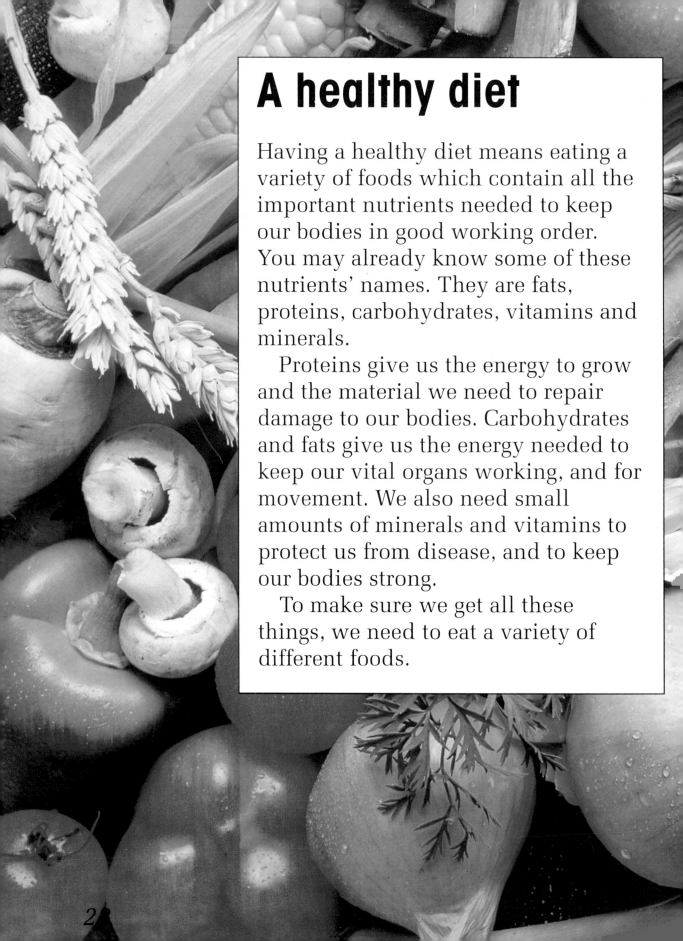

A healthy diet

Having a healthy diet means eating a variety of foods which contain all the important nutrients needed to keep our bodies in good working order. You may already know some of these nutrients' names. They are fats, proteins, carbohydrates, vitamins and minerals.

Proteins give us the energy to grow and the material we need to repair damage to our bodies. Carbohydrates and fats give us the energy needed to keep our vital organs working, and for movement. We also need small amounts of minerals and vitamins to protect us from disease, and to keep our bodies strong.

To make sure we get all these things, we need to eat a variety of different foods.

This picture shows some of the most important nutrients in food, and explains why our bodies need them.

Vitamin A is good for our eyes, bones and teeth. The best foods for vitamin A are vegetables, particularly carrots.

Vitamin B helps to build a healthy blood supply. It is found in eggs, meat and dairy produce.

Iron also helps our blood to stay healthy. Green vegetables such as cabbage and broccoli are excellent sources of iron.

Carbohydrates are dissolved by our bodies and can be turned into energy-giving glucose. Vegetables, pasta and bread are good sources of carbohydrates.

Proteins build muscles and help our vital organs to stay in good repair. Fish, meat, pulses, rice and dairy products are rich in protein.

Vitamin C is needed to keep our bones and skin healthy. It also helps us to fight illness. Citrus fruits such as lemons and oranges are a good source of vitamin C.

Calcium keeps our bones and teeth strong. Milk and green vegetables contain a lot of calcium.

23

Mouthwatering!

OPPOSITE Look at this tasty burger! Think about biting into it. . . . Has your mouth started to water?

For most of us, sitting down to our favourite meal is something to look forward to, but what makes a meal our favourite?

Our senses play an important part in getting us ready to eat food. First of all, a meal needs to look attractive and smell appetizing. The look and smell of food triggers off **glands**, which produce saliva in our mouths. When this happens we say that our mouths are watering. What is really happening is that our mouths are getting ready to receive food.

See for yourself
There are four groups of food tastes: bitter, sour, salty and sweet. You can investigate how your sense of taste is linked to sight and smell.

You will need a selection of different foods (such as cheese, jam, apple, onion, yoghurt, orange, tomato, chocolate and lemon), some friends, some plates and covers for the food.

1. Blindfold some friends and allow them to taste a little piece of each food, whilst holding their nose. Can they name the foods and put them into taste groups?

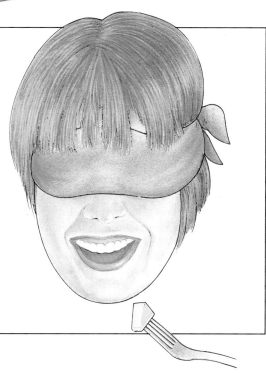

2. Now try a second tasting using all the senses. Can they put the foods into taste groups now?

Digestion

Mouth and Teeth
Teeth and saliva break down the food by chewing. The food is swallowed as a bolus.

Oesophagus
The bolus of food is squeezed down the oesophagus into the stomach.

Stomach
In the stomach acid is added to the food to break it down even further.

Small Intestine
A long narrow tube where the food is mixed with digestive juices to make a soup-like liquid. The body begins to absorb all the nutrients it needs from this liquid.

Large Intestine
A long wide tube where more nutrients are absorbed. Water is also removed from the food. What is left passes out through the anus as faeces.

Rectum

Anus

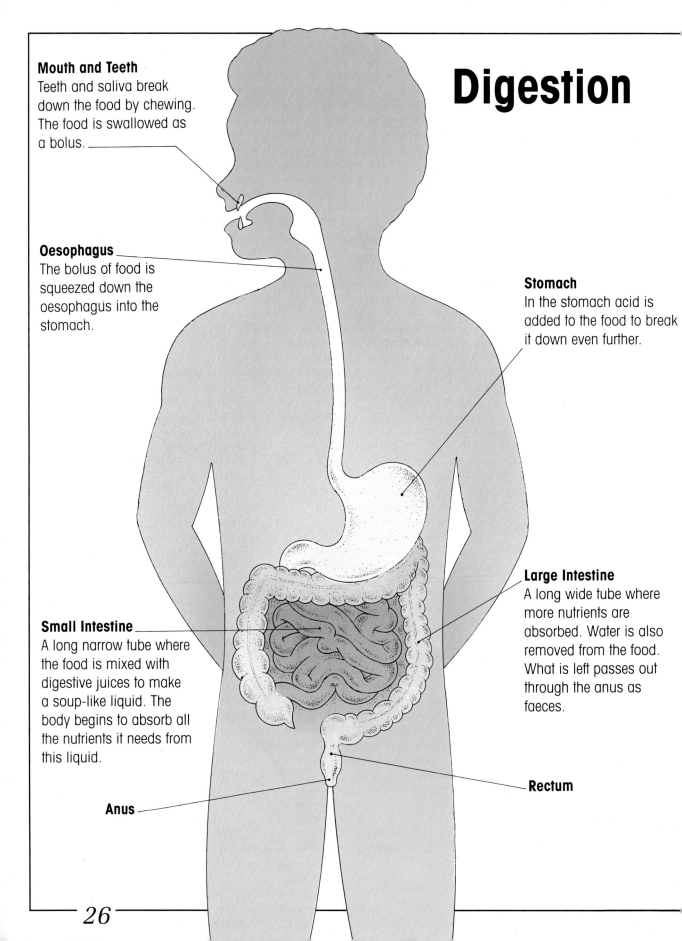

Before your body can use the nutrients in your food to do important jobs, your meal must first be digested. This means that it is gradually broken down into tiny bits that your body can use. The parts of your body which do this job are known as the digestive system. The breaking down of the food is called digestion.

Digestion starts as soon as food enters your mouth and you chew it. Digestion ends when the waste (the parts of the food which your body cannot use) leaves your body through the **anus** when you go to the toilet. The passage from the mouth to the anus is called the alimentary canal.

Food takes about twenty hours to travel all the way through the alimentary canal. As the food passes through, it is broken down into a soup-like liquid and the important nutrients are **absorbed** into the body.

The digestive process starts as soon as food enters your mouth and you chew. Your teeth crush the food, whilst saliva starts to break it down even further.

The waste system

If you want to be fit and healthy it is essential that your digestive system is working well. Eating plenty of fibre and exercising regularly will help to keep your digestive system in good order.

Not all of the food we eat is used by our bodies. When digestion has finished, waste food passes along the large intestine and forms into **faeces**. The faeces collects in the **rectum**, before it is passed out of the body through the anus when we go to the toilet. The diagram on page 26 of the digestive system will show you where all these parts of the body are. Faeces contains poisons, or toxins. It is important that your waste system works well, so that it can get rid of these toxins from your body as quickly as possible.

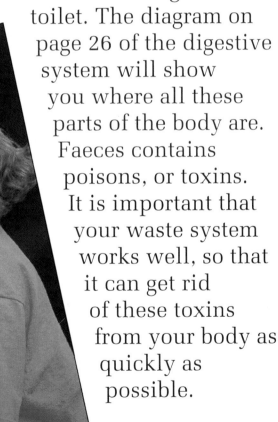

To help keep your waste system working properly, it is a good idea to eat plenty of foods which contain **fibre**. Fibre gives more bulk to the waste, and so helps it pass along the large intestine more easily.

Most liquid waste is passed through our **kidneys** and is stored in the **bladder**, until we need to go to the toilet. Our body gets rid of liquid waste as **urine**.

When fresh food is processed a lot of the fibre it contains is removed. Wholemeal bread is made from flour which has not been processed. It still contains much of its fibre.

Glossary

Absorbed   Soaked up.

Anus   A small opening at the end of the alimentary canal, where solid waste leaves the body.

Bacteria   Very small organisms that are all around us. Some make living things decay.

Bladder   The part of your body that holds liquid waste (urine) until it is ready to leave your body when you go to the toilet.

Carbon dioxide   One of the many gases in the air. You cannot see it.

Chemicals   Chemical is the general scientific name for many of the different substances in the world around us. Salt, sugar and lemon juice are all chemicals.

Climate   The weather conditions in a certain place.

Destroy   To kill something.

Faeces   The solid waste that is produced when food is digested.

Fibre   Something found in food which our digestive system cannot break down. It passes right through the body and comes out in faeces when we go to the toilet.

Food producers   All the people who are involved in making the food that you buy at the shops.

Fungi   A kind of plant which does not make its food using sunlight.

Glands   Special parts of your body which produce important substances, such as saliva.

Hygienic   Clean.

Kidneys   One of the vital organs in your body. Their job is to help get rid of the urine that is made when your meal is digested.

Mineral salts Substances which are needed to protect our bodies, and make them work well.

Nutrients Special things that are found in food. They are used by our bodies to do all sorts of very important jobs.

Preserved To have stopped something from decaying.

Rectum The end of the alimentary canal.

Refrigerated When something is very cold. Refrigerated lorries and containers keep food cold, to stop it from decaying.

Starches A food that plants make by photosynthesis.

Sterile Without germs.

Temperatures How hot or cold something is.

Urine The liquid waste that is produced when food and drink are digested.

Vital organs All the important organs inside our bodies, such as the heart and lungs.

Further Reading

The *Food Facts* series (Wayland, 1992)
Diet by Brian Ward (Franklin Watts, 1991)
Food by Kay Davies and Wendy Oldfield (Wayland, 1991)
Food by Terry Jennings (Oxford University Press, 1984)

Picture acknowledgements

All Sport 23; Bruce Coleman 13, 16; Cephas 5, 6, 7; Eye Ubiquitous 16, 29; Images 28; Life File 25; Science Photo Library 4, 12, 23; Tony Stone 10, 11, 13, 19, 20; Swift 6; WPL 5, 21; Zefa 18; Zul Mukhida 15. The artwork on pages 10-11 is by Peter Bull.

Index